D0604895

CHESSIE, THE TRAVELIN' MAN

WRITTEN by: Randy Houk

ILLUSTRATED by: Paula Bartlett

for Chip and Judi, devotedly
~ Randy Houk

with love and appreciation for my best
friends; mom, dad and Stephen
~ Paula Bartlett

HSUS The Humane Society of
the United States

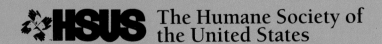

Long ago, in southern seas
There were many manatees.
Called 'sea cows', for their round shapes,
They ate sea grass and sea grapes.

Shy and gentle, friendly too,
Sea cows' enemies were few.
Back when Pirates sailed the seas,
It was safe for manatees.

Sometimes sailors thought they'd seen
Some pale, drifting mermaid queen.
But as far as we can tell,
They could not see very well.

Each time, it turned out to be
Just another manatee:
Gray and rounded, long and slow,
Flippers moving to and fro.

3

*P*irate ships no longer roam
Near the sea cows' southern home.
Motorboats and speedboats race,
Taking up a lot of space.

Sharp propellers slice just where
Sea cows must come up for air.
Criss-cross scars are plain to see
On an adult manatee.

Now, where manatees were many
There are really hardly any,
Sixteen hundred at a guess:
Some say there are even less.

One Spring day just recently,
As a breeze blew pleasantly,
Sparkles danced upon the bay.
Ripples made the sea grass sway.

One brown pelican flew by,
Dark against a hazy sky.
Patterns shifted in the sea,
All around a manatee.

She was nearly ten feet long,
Six years old, and very strong.
She was twisting to and fro,
Stirring up the sand below.

Then the mother manatee
Pushed her calf into the sea.
He bumped right against her side.
When she rose, he stayed beside.

Whiskery noses, in a pair
Surfaced for a gulp of air.
Even though the calf was new
He knew just what he should do.

Near his mother's flipper, he
Nursed and drank milk hungrily.
He nursed while she watched with pride,
Drifting gently, side by side.

Several sunlit weeks flew past.
That calf nursed and he grew fast.
Summer brought the hotter weather,
Still the pair stayed close together.

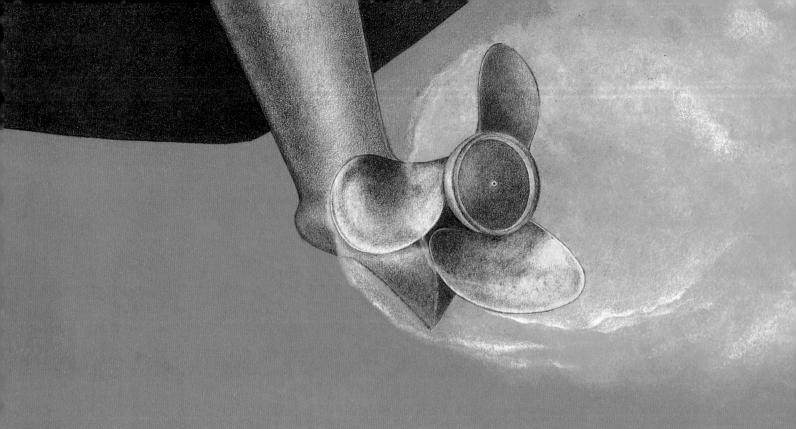

One late lazy afternoon,
Somewhere toward the end of June,
Mother manatee could hear
Buzzing sounds, from somewhere near.

She began to push her son.
He mistook her fear for fun.
Then there was an awful 'thump',
Followed by another 'bump'.

He was hurt, which made him duck.
That was smart, or just good luck.
Though his cut back made him squeal,
He was young and he would heal.

11

In just two years, he was grown.
He spent lots of time alone,
Though he'd sometimes play and nuzzle
Near a friendly sea cow's muzzle.

Like so many sea cows, he
Had a lot of scars to see.
He had learned when boats were near,
Manatees had best steer clear.

Near the Barrier waterway
He would feed and rest and play.
Near the power plants he'd go.
He would surf the warm outflow.

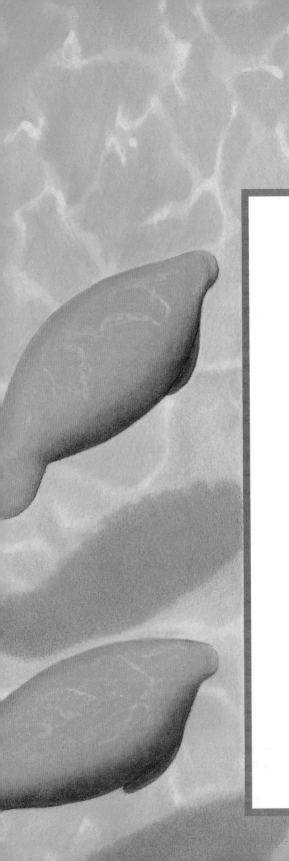

$\mathcal{J}$une of nineteen-ninety four
Was a scorcher, that's for sure.
Folks ashore held hoses out
For a curious sea cow snout.

Our calf pushed his whiskered nose
Right up to a rubber hose.
Cool, fresh water was a treat:
Thirst-quenching and very sweet.

Probably, the heat that season
Gave our manatee a reason
With some others, to set forth:
It was cooler in the North.

Finding cooler water, most
Stopped to feed along the coast.
Rarely does a sea cow roam
Very far away from home.

But our manatee kept on.
He seemed somehow to be drawn.
He swam thirty miles a day,
Ate and rested on the way.

15

Near Virginia's Eastern Shore,
Our sea cow was seen once more
Munching grass and vegetation
In a salty marsh location.

By July, he'd made his way
Up into the Chesapeake Bay.
This is where he got his name:
He gained quite a bit of fame.

"Chessie is a travelin' man,"
One newspaper's story ran.
Chessie seemed to like the Bay:
He showed no desire to stray.

August came, and August went.
Much to folks' astonishment,
Even with a brisk breeze blowing
Chessie showed no signs of going.

This caused experts some alarm.
Winter's cold would do him harm,
If the water went below
Sixty-eight degrees or so.

"Save our Chessie," T-shirts said.
"If he stays, he'll soon be dead."
"That would be an awful pity,"
Said the manatee committee.

Late that fall, an expert team
Hung their nets to block a stream
Flowing down into the bay.
Chessie tried to get away.

It took hours, but they caught him.
Carried in a sling they brought him,
Six men got him in the plane,
For the flight back home again.

Safe in Florida once more,
In the shallows just offshore,
Chessie got a radio tag,
A transmitter he would drag.

20

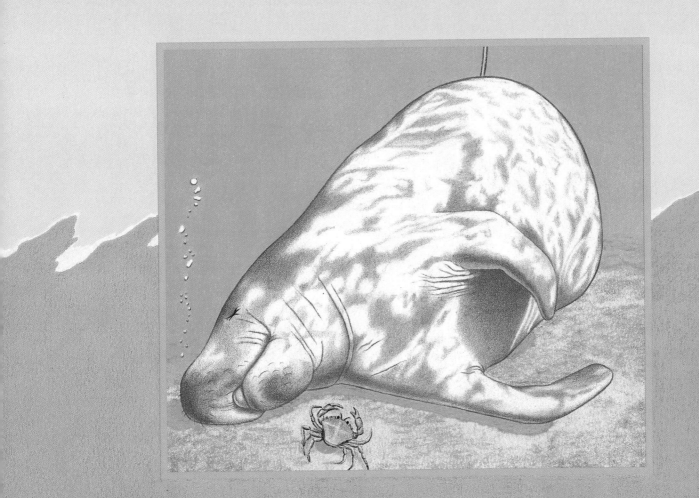

This would signal, and would show
When he traveled, where he'd go.
After that, he swam away,
Down the shallow Waterway.

Through the cold of February,
In a shallow estuary,
Chessie dozed and dreamed and ate.
He was quite content to wait.

But in June just like before,
North he went, along the shore.
He swam steadily each day,
Acting like he knew the way:

Past Savannah, Georgia where
Manatees were very rare,
Past the graceful Charleston Bay,
Where the Spanish mosses sway.

Up past Myrtle Beach he swam
Just as though he had a plan.
Near Cape Hatteras he was seen
Just beyond a putting green.

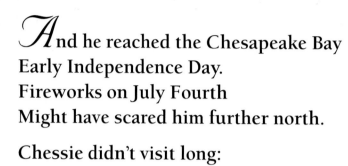

And he reached the Chesapeake Bay
Early Independence Day.
Fireworks on July Fourth
Might have scared him further north.

Chessie didn't visit long:
Past Cape May he moved along.
He swam past Atlantic City,
Where the beaches are so pretty.

Late that month he reached New York,
Where he took a left-hand fork,
Stopping briefly, just to see
The Statue of Liberty.

Warmer waters Chessie found
Following Long Island Sound.
In the shallow Dolphin's Cove,
He was spotted, as he dove.

Someone saw him close to Yale
(But mistook him for a whale).
Never had a sea cow strayed
This far from Port Everglade.

And by August twenty-four
Folks were worrying once more.
Chessie showed no sign of turning,
Which to experts, was concerning.

Down in Florida, some folk
Thought the worry was a joke.
"All this fuss - ridiculous!
Watch - he'll just swim back to us."

It turned out that they were right:
No one need have taken fright.
Near Point Judith colder weather
Stopped his progress altogether.

Fifteen hundred miles he'd come.
Now his nose was growing numb.
In the icy surf offshore,
Chessie headed South once more.

No one had to interfere:
Chessie's plan was very clear.
Pointing south, he just kept going,
Swimming daily, without slowing.

Near New Haven, Chessie felt
Drag on his transmitter belt.
The transmitter came unsnapped:
He pulled loose, and wasn't trapped.

Someone surfing had a shock
In New Jersey, near a dock.
Chessie surfaced in the foam,
Right beside him, swimming home.

Past Cape May and Assateague,
Past Onley and Wachapreague,
Past Barco and Cape Romain,
Chessie swam back home again.

By October, he was back,
Not one new scar on his back,
Spotted just near Jacksonville,
Not a bit fatigued or ill.

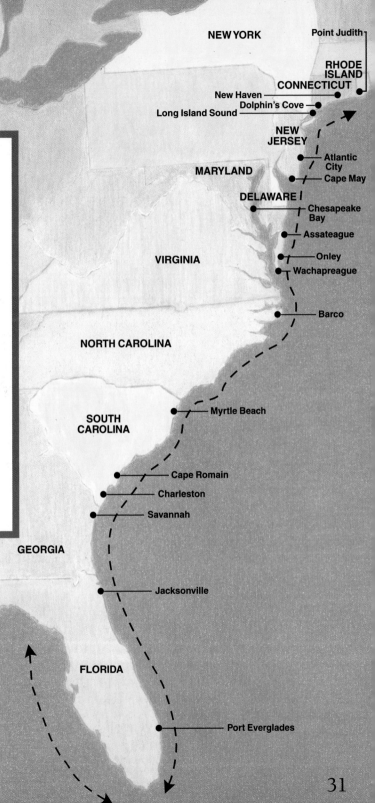

What would make a manatee
Practice such insanity?
What made Chessie choose to go?
We can't answer: we don't know.

Possibly one day he just
Got a case of wanderlust.
No sea cow has done what he did:
Chessie tried and he succeeded.

If one day, you see him floating
Right beside you, when you're boating,
Please remember to take care:
Manatees are growing rare.

Glossary

Roam	Wander, go away from
Propellers	Blades of a motor on a boat
Muzzle	The nose and snout of an animal
Outflow	The warm water currents from a power plant
Scorcher	A very hot day
Thirst-Quenching	Drinking enough to end the need for more
Vegetation	Green growing things
Location	A place
Astonishment	Surprise
Estuary	Area where a river meets the sea or ocean
Ridiculous	Silly, foolish
Interfere	Get in the way
Fatigued	Tired, weary
Ill	Sick
Wanderlust	The desire to roam, travel

The real Chessie

Special thanks to the Sirenia Project, U.S. Department of the Interior, and the U.S. Fish and Wildlife Service for their help in researching the story of Chessie the manatee.

Special thanks to Save the Manatee® Club for providing information on Chessie the manatee. If you would like to find out more information on manatees or SMC's Adopt-A-Manatee program, please contact:

Save the Manatee® Club
500 N. Maitland Avenue
Maitland, FL 32751
1-800-432-JOIN (5646)
or access them on the Internet at:
http://www.objectlinks.com/manatee

The Humane Society of the United States, a nonprofit organization founded in 1954, and with a constituency of over 3.5 million persons, is dedicated to speaking for animals, who cannot speak for themselves. The HSUS is devoted to making the world safe for animals through legal, educational, legislative and investigative means. The HSUS believes that humans have a moral obligation to protect other species with which we share the Earth. Co-sponsorship of this book by The Humane Society of the United States does not imply any partnership, joint venture, or other direct affiliation between The HSUS and the Sirenia Project, USFWS or Save the Manatee® Club. For information on The HSUS, call: (202) 452-1100.

Originally published by The Benefactory, Inc., One Post Road, Fairfield, CT 06430. The Benefactory produces books, tapes and toys that foster animal protection and environmental preservation. Call (203) 255-7744. This edition is published by Reader's Digest Young Families, Inc., Westport, CT 06880. Text Copyright©1997 Randy Houk. Illustrations copyright©1997 The Benefactory, Inc. Designed by Anita Soos Design, Inc. Printed in Italy.